D1271464

MINNESOTA
VIKINGS

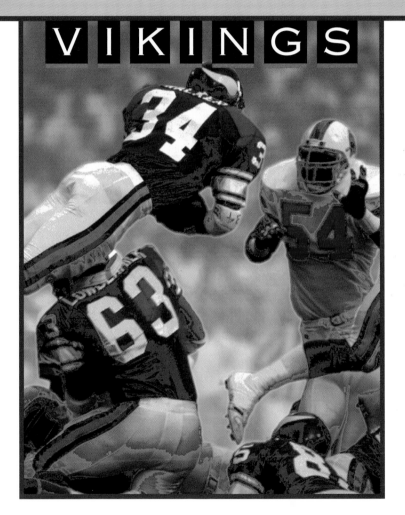

STEVE POTTS

CREATIVE EDUCATION INC.

Published by Creative Education, Inc.
123 S. Broad Street, Mankato, Minnesota 56001

Designed by Rita Marshall
Cover illustration by Lance Hidy Associates
Photos by Sportschrome, Allsport, Bettmann Archives,
Wide World Photos, Duomo, Third Coast,
Strictly Sports, Spectra-Action and Focus on Sports

Library of Congress Cataloging-in-Publication Data

Potts, Steve.
  Minnesota Vikings/Steve Potts.
  p. cm.
  ISBN 0-88682-374-9
  1. Minnesota Vikings (Football team)—History. I. Title.
GV956.M5P68 1990
796.332'64'09776579—dc20   90-41528
                                             CIP

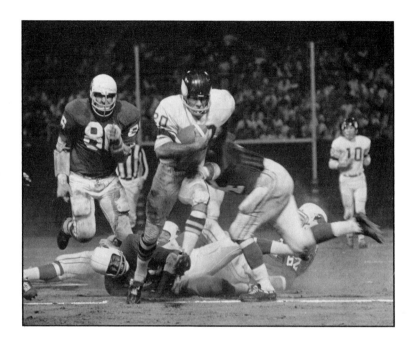

Each winter snow and cold descend on Minnesota like a blanket, wrapping this frigid northern state until the warm sun of spring heats the frozen land. Not many people are hardy enough to brave the cold. Among the hardiest people who do, however, are the fans of Minnesota's winter-loving pro football team, the Minnesota Vikings.

Minnesota might seem like an unlikely place for a pro football team, but the team's original founder, Max Winter, was determined to bring professional sports to his adopted home, Minnesota's Twin Cities (St. Paul and Minneapolis). Born in Austria, Winter was not very familiar with American sports. But after he had been in this country

Running back Tommy Mason scored the lone Viking touchdown in an early contest with Baltimore.

for several years, he grew to love basketball. As his business prospered, he used his earnings to found the Minneapolis Lakers in 1947, a professional basketball team that would eventually move to Los Angeles.

It wasn't until 1955 that Max Winter saw his first football game. He was captivated by all of the excitement it generated, and decided that football was more fun than basketball. Winter began writing many letters to the NFL commissioner asking for a football franchise for Minnesota, but his letters went unanswered. He was almost ready to join the newly founded American Football League in 1959 when the NFL announced in January 1960 that Minnesota and Max Winter finally would be getting a pro football team. Minnesotans were thrilled! Residents of the "Land of 10,000 Lakes" would now have pro football *and* basketball teams to root for.

Max Winter was determined to hire the best talent possible for his new team, and he began with his coach. Winter first offered the job to a young coach, Harry Peter "Bud" Grant, who had also played on Winter's Minneapolis Lakers basketball team. When Grant turned him down, Winter hired Norm Van Brocklin in 1961. At only thirty-six years of age, Van Brocklin, or "The Dutchman" as he was called, was the youngest coach in the NFL. But Van Brocklin, who coached the Vikings from 1961 to 1966, brought a wealth of experience to his new position. He had been a quarterback for the Los Angeles Rams and the Philadelphia Eagles. The Eagles had gone to the NFL championship game in 1960, partly because of Van Brocklin's talents as a quarterback. Now Van Brocklin was looking forward to the chance to coach.

Unfortunately, however, it wasn't everything he

Chris Doleman (#56), a Viking star for the nineties.

expected. While he had lots of experience dealing with the game, Van Brocklin didn't deal well with his players. He had a horrible temper and often exploded in anger at his young team. "I thought you guys could win," Van Brocklin said once, "but I guess I was wrong." Many of the players came to resent and dislike their loud, demanding coach.

Defensive end Jim Marshall started an incredible nineteen-year career with the Vikings.

TARKENTON AND THE EARLY YEARS

The first Vikings' team was a mix of tested old veterans and untried new players. After three seasons with losing records—1961 (3-11), 1962 (2-11-1), and 1963 (5-8-1)—many of the team's fans were beginning to wonder what was wrong with the Vikings. By the time the team had its first winning season in 1964, four of the young Vikings—Bill Brown, Fred Cox, Jim Marshall, and Francis Tarkenton—had shaped the club into a serious threat.

Most football teams seem to rally naturally around the quarterback, and the Vikings were no exception. Francis Asbury Tarkenton, better known to Minnesota fans as "Fran" or "the Tark," was one of the Vikings' first draftees. This young southerner fired the imaginations of Minnesota fans and players alike. Tarkenton was born in Richmond, Virginia in 1940. The son of a minister, he was a sickly boy as a child. He suffered from asthma, a disease that left him gasping for breath after exercising. Most people thought that Fran's asthma would ruin his chance to play in school sports. Tarkenton, however, showed the same strength that would later be so valuable on the football field; he recovered from his asthma, and when his family moved to Athens, Georgia, he eventually found a football team to play with there.

Football wasn't Tarkenton's only love, though. He also played baseball and basketball, sports that made him a high school hero. While he was recruited by many colleges, he decided to enroll at his hometown school upon graduation from high school. The University of Georgia in Athens had a fine football program, and Tarkenton hoped that he could continue to play while he received a good education.

It was at Georgia that he began developing the unique style, dubbed "scrambling" by sportswriters, that he would later introduce to the NFL. Instead of waiting to be sacked by the opposing defensive line, Tarkenton ran, dodged, and wove around the backfield, buying time to set up the perfect pass. The strategy was often successful. As a result he frequently passed for long yardage and often for a touchdown. His ability to protect himself while he delivered passes with deadly accuracy made him very attractive to the Vikings, who needed a quarterback who could manage on his own until the Vikings established a strong offensive line.

Tarkenton's talents were showcased in his first game in a Vikings' uniform, in which Minnesota was meeting its archrivals, the Chicago Bears. The Bears, who looked down on this ragtag new team, expected to win easily. Instead, they found themselves facing a young rookie quarterback who had no intention of losing. Tossing four passes for touchdowns and running one touchdown in himself, Tarkenton led his team to a 37-13 upset win over the humiliated Bears. Since this was the team's first regular-season game played before the home crowd in the Twin Cities, Minnesotans soon developed an intense interest in and respect for Fran Tarkenton.

1 9 6 2

Fran Tarkenton's innovative scrambling was one of the strengths of the Viking offense.

Another Georgia Bulldog turned Viking, Herschel Walker (#34).
(pages 10–11)

Carl Eller, a five-time All Pro defensive end, was the Vikings' number one draft pick.

All of Tarkenton's moments in a Vikings' uniform were not so pleasant. Under Coach Van Brocklin, the team see-sawed from losing to winning to losing, and from running to passing to running. Van Brocklin blamed Tarkenton for the team's losses, complaining that the quarterback needed to adopt a new style of passing. After one game he told Tarkenton, "You're not strong enough to throw passes like that. But you sure are dumb enough." Such abuse angered Tarkenton and the other young players, and many demanded to be traded. Tarkenton got his wish in 1966, when he left to join the New York Giants. Van Brocklin left too, leaving both players and fans furious at the temperamental coach.

While many fans adopted Tarkenton as the symbol for their young team, football is a team effort, and no one realized that more than Fran Tarkenton. He owed much of his success to those teammates—including Bill Brown, Fred Cox, and Jim Marshall—who helped shape the Vikings into a major force to be reckoned with in the NFL's Central Division.

Many of Fran Tarkenton's passes found their way into the arms of Bill Brown, who ended up playing for Minnesota for thirteen seasons (1962–1974). Brown came to Minnesota as part of the NFL's expansion team program. Originally, he had been drafted out of Illinois by the Chicago Bears, but stiff competition for that team's running back slots meant that he saw little action. That changed once he was a Viking. Brown piled up 9,200 yards rushing during his stunning NFL career. And from 1964 to 1966 he was the Vikings' leading rusher.

When Tarkenton couldn't move the ball in the air, Fred Cox, the Vikings' kicker, was often called on to produce a miracle with his well-aimed kicks, and he usually did. Cox had gone to the Cleveland Browns from the University of Pittsburgh in 1961. After playing for the Browns, he was traded to Minnesota, where he started as the Vikings' placekicker for fifteen seasons (1963–1977). The team leader in points scored from 1963 to 1973, he often put himself in the record books with seasons in which he had over one hundred points. He also led the NFL in points kicked in 1969 and 1970. A career total of 1,365 points scored places Cox among the NFL's all-time best kickers. Cox, like Fran Tarkenton and many of the other Vikings, spent his off-seasons working at another job. Cox moved his young family to Buffalo, Minnesota, a small town near the Twin Cities, where he farmed and worked as a chiropractor.

1 9 6 6

Dave Osborn ran for big yardage during the Vikings' 20-17 upset over NFL champion Green Bay.

All of a quarterback's best efforts are worthless if his team's defense can't stop the opposing club. Fran Tarkenton was blessed with one of the league's best defensemen in his friend Jim Marshall. Marshall, who occupied the defensive end spot on the Vikings' line for a remarkable nineteen seasons, seemed to defy injury and illness. This 6'4", 240-pound wonder started in 222 consecutive games, every Minnesota game for over fifteen seasons. "With my mind and body working together," Marshall said, "I can accomplish much more than I would trying to work strictly on the physical or the mental planes. I think it is this harmony within me that enables me to continue playing even under very adverse conditions." Whatever the explanation for his good health, Marshall proved to be one of the team's most consistent and valuable members.

Vikings' fans loved to watch Marshall play, although some of them also remembered the embarrassing and

1 9 6 7

Bud Grant became the coach of the Vikings—a position he would hold for eighteen seasons.

humorous slipup he had made early in his career. In an October 1964 game against the San Francisco 49ers, Marshall recovered a fumble, jumped away from his opponents' grasp, turned, and headed down the field, running sixty-six yards into the end zone for a touchdown. As he congratulated himself, he noticed that the fans were laughing and the players, both the 49ers and the Vikings, were smiling and gesturing. To his horror and surprise, he soon realized that he had run the ball into the wrong end zone! The Vikings went on to win the game anyway, and, although Marshall was teased about his error, it was a very rare mistake in a long and exciting football career.

THE GLORY YEARS, 1967–1978

The departure of coach and quarterback in 1966 meant that there were changes in the wind for the Vikings. When Norm Van Brocklin left at the end of the 1966 season, there was only one man Max Winter wanted to coach his team: Bud Grant. Although Grant had turned Winter's offer down in 1961, he accepted it in 1967, and a long, happy, and successful relationship began between an amazing coach and an amazing team.

Bud Grant came to the Vikings with a long, impressive resume. After dropping out of the University of Minnesota after his senior football season, Grant joined Max Winter's Minneapolis Lakers, a team that eventually won two National Basketball Association titles. After a successful career on the courts, Grant began an even more successful career on the gridiron, joining the Philadelphia Eagles in 1951. He later played for, then coached, the Winnipeg Blue Bombers in the Canadian Football League, leading the

Like Wade Wilson (#11), Bud Grant turned Minnesota upside down.

The Hero: The Vikings defeated Green Bay 9-7 on the strength of three Fred Cox field goals.

team to four league championships in ten years. By the time he retired in 1986, Grant had coached for twenty-eight years, eighteen of them with the Vikings, and had 270 career victories in the CFL and NFL. Today he ranks seventh on the NFL's all-time coaching victories list.

Nearly everyone who worked with Bud Grant praised his quiet winning formula. Unlike Van Brocklin, Grant rarely yelled at his players. Fran Tarkenton said of his longtime friend, "The secret of this team's success can be traced right to Bud Grant. He's the catalyst who has put it all together with good trades, good draft choices, and very good coaching. I've learned more from him than anybody I've ever been associated with—in or out of football." Grant's philosophy was simple: do the best you can. He had a healthy approach to something that is a disappointment to all coaches: losing. "It's the losses that haunt you," Grant admitted, "but in this business, you've got to try to get over those losses if you're going to maintain your sanity."

In his eighteen years as Vikings coach (1967 to 1983 and 1985), Grant was blessed with one of football's best defensive lines, the group of players that came to be known as the "Purple People Eaters," or simply "The Purple Gang." The two mainstays of the defensive line were defensive end Carl Eller and defensive tackle Alan Page, men who came to be dreaded throughout the league for their ability to stop just about anything that was thrown at them.

Carl Eller, at 6'6" and 265 pounds, was an imposing and feared figure in the NFL. Minnesota's first-round draft choice in 1964, Eller played for the Vikings until 1978. His Vikings' teammates best remember him for his halftime pep talk during the December 22, 1973, playoff game with

A mainstay of the Viking offense in the 1970s, Sammy White (#85).

Joey Browner carried on the "Purple People Eater" tradition in the 1990s.

Alan Page, the most feared defensive tackle in the NFL, blocked six kicks during the season.

the Washington Redskins. With the Redskins holding a 7-3 lead at the half, Eller stomped into the dressing room, dumped the contents off a table, and threw a chalkboard across the room. There was complete silence. Eller was furious. "Don't think about anything but hitting," he warned. "If we hit, we win. Any of you who don't feel like hitting, just stay in here and let the rest of us go out and finish the game." The talk worked. The Vikings left the locker room yelling. Charged up, they rushed onto the field and rolled over the Redskins during the second half, beating them 27-20.

Alan Page, the first defensive player in the NFL to be named Most Valuable Player (1971), joined the Vikings in 1967 and played for the Purple Gang until 1978. An All-American at Notre Dame, Page demonstrated what he could do on the field during his second game as a freshman with the Fighting Irish. Early in the game he picked up a blocked punt, ran it down the field for fifty-seven yards, brushed off everyone who stood in his way, and scored a touchdown against Purdue. Notre Dame coach Ara Parseghian got so excited that he somersaulted down the sidelines and into the end zone. Page's continued success as a pro often provoked comments and elicited praise from his teammates. One of them remarked that "if he gets a hand on somebody, he generally brings them down." Vikings' linebacker Lonnie Warwick added that Page was "the best football player I've ever seen or ever will see."

So much attention was given to the Vikings' defense that the superb offense was often overlooked. But center Mick Tingelhoff was one player whose contributions were appreciated by all his teammates. Although he was passed up in the college draft when he graduated from Nebraska, he was good enough to be offered contracts by the CFL's Calgary team and the NFL's St. Louis team as well as by the Vikings. Tingelhoff chose the Vikings. A seventeen-year career, an incredible fourteen years with no missed games, and a spot on the NFL All-Pro team from 1964 to 1970 was the result. Though centers usually don't get much recognition, quarterbacks know how valuable a good center can be. Fran Tarkenton said of his protector, "There aren't more than three or four guys in the history of the game who have had the kind of career at his position that Mick has."

1 9 7 3

The Vikings drafted running back Chuck Foreman, who soon developed into a consistent 1000-yard rusher.

This wealth of talent, and the contributions of Vikings Paul Krause, Gary Larsen, Doug Sutherland, and Wally Hilgenberg, came together to give the Vikings winning seasons in 1968 (8-6), 1969 (12-2), 1970 (12-2), and 1971 (11-3), as well as ten Central Division championships (1968 to 1971 and 1973 to 1978), four National Football League and Conference crowns (1969, 1973, 1974, and 1976), and numerous playoff appearances. But in the early 1970s there was something lacking: a consistent quarterback.

After Fran Tarkenton left in 1966, the Vikings went through quarterback after quarterback. No one seemed to click with the strong offensive line and the Bud Grant style. Joe Kapp was lured away from the Canadian Football League in 1967 and stayed with the Vikings for two seasons. He had some brilliant moments, such as the seven touchdowns passes he threw in a game against the Baltimore Colts on September 28, 1969, but he was inconsistent. Bud Grant was anxious to try a reliable passing game behind a strong-armed quarterback. Who better for this job than Fran Tarkenton?

Tarkenton had not enjoyed many successful or happy

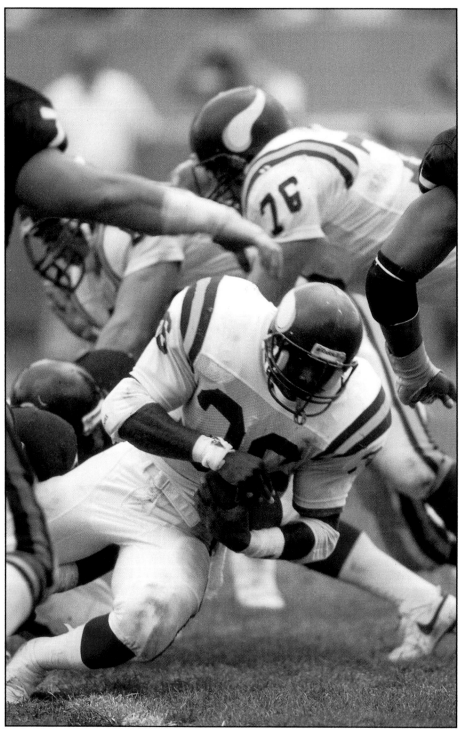

The tough and dependable Allen Rice (#36).

moments since he had been traded to the New York Giants, and knowing that Bud Grant wanted him back convinced him to ask for a trade. In 1972, Tarkenton came home to Minnesota.

The team that Tarkenton returned to seemed electrified by his homecoming. In the next four years, the Vikings made it to the Super Bowl three times. For Tarkenton, however, the records weren't that important. "The records are secondary to what our team does. I'm more concerned with things other than statistical charts. Was I an asset to my team? Did I successfully display the leadership qualities a quarterback is supposed to have?" The fans and players thought he did. In 1975 he was named the NFL's Most Valuable Player, and was selected by his fellow players to receive the Jim Thorpe Award, an honor bestowed by pro football players on the one who exemplifies the best in the sport.

Although Tarkenton's return and the combination of a potent offense and a spirited defense meant numerous NFC Central titles and four NFC championships, the biggest prize of all still eluded the Vikings. Bud Grant coached his team to four Super Bowls, but the Vikings could not produce a victory in any of them. How could they fail to win the world championship?

No one seemed to know, least of all the Vikings. They had a fine offense and defense, superb coaching, and excellent morale, but still they lost: 23-7 to the Kansas City Chiefs (1970), 24-7 to the Miami Dolphins (1974), 16-6 to the Pittsburgh Steelers (1975), and 32-14 to the Oakland Raiders (1976). The losses hurt, especially the last since the Purple People Eaters were beginning to break up as a

1 9 7 4

Tark's number 1! Phenomenal quarterback Fran Tarkenton led the league in touchdown passes.

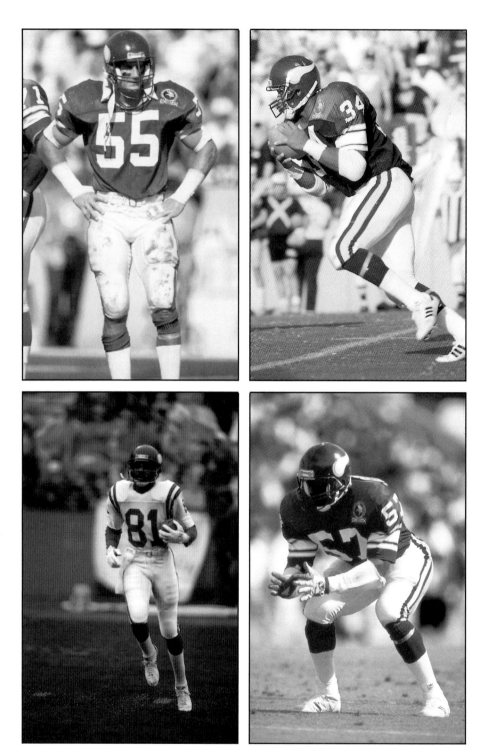

Clockwise: Scott Studwell, Herschel Walker, Mike Merriweather, Anthony Carter.

result of trades, injuries, and retirements. Although Bud Grant continued to coach until 1985, things just weren't the same. The glory years were over.

THE VIKINGS REBUILD

The opening of the new Hubert Humphrey Metrodome in April 1982 signaled a new era for the Vikings. The old Met, Metropolitan Stadium, was gone, and so were Tarkenton, Chuck Foreman, Ahmad Rashad, Eller, Page, and the rest of the Purple Gang of the 1970s. The team was sporting a new stadium, but it was also showing off a new roster, a roster that promised to usher in a new generation of Vikings' heroes.

1 9 8 8

Defensive tackle Keith Millard was tops among Minnesota's linemen with seventy solo tackles.

With the retirement of the Purple People Eaters, a new generation of Vikings' defensive talent was born through drafts and trades. Doug Martin, Matt Blair, and Scott Studwell strengthened the Vikings' defensive squad. Martin, a defensive end, was a leading tackler and aided in quarterback sacks. As a ten-year veteran, he added a measure of stability to a young team. Matt Blair played for twelve seasons as a Viking linebacker. His teammate Scott Studwell led the Vikings in tackles for seven seasons, making the Pro Bowl team in 1987 and 1988. But despite the addition of fine defensive players like these the Vikings' fortunes tumbled. In 1984 the club hit rockbottom. Under the direction of Les Steckel, who had replaced Bud Grant after the 1983 season, the club had its worst record in almost twenty years. A change was badly needed.

Unexpectedly the change came in the form of a familiar face, "the Old Trapper" himself, Bud Grant. Grant would only coach Minnesota for one additional season, but he

Two Viking standouts of the nineties, Wade Wilson (#11) and Rick Fenney (#31). (pages 26–27)

redirected the ship and left the wheel in capable hands. The new captain for the 1986 season and into the 1990s would be Jerry Burns, who had been an assistant under Grant for twenty years.

With Burns at the helm the Vikings brought in an entire new cast of characters. Keith Millard, Chris Doleman, Joey Browner, Steve Jordan, Wade Wilson, Gary Zimmerman, Carl Lee and Randall McDaniel would each become all-pros under "Burnsie's" watchful eye.

But of all these talented players, the most exciting might have been Anthony Carter. This energetic wide receiver came to the Vikings from the United States Football League in 1985. A three-time All-American at the University of Michigan, whom Bo Schembechler called, "The greatest athlete I've ever coached," quickly established himself as a Viking superstar.

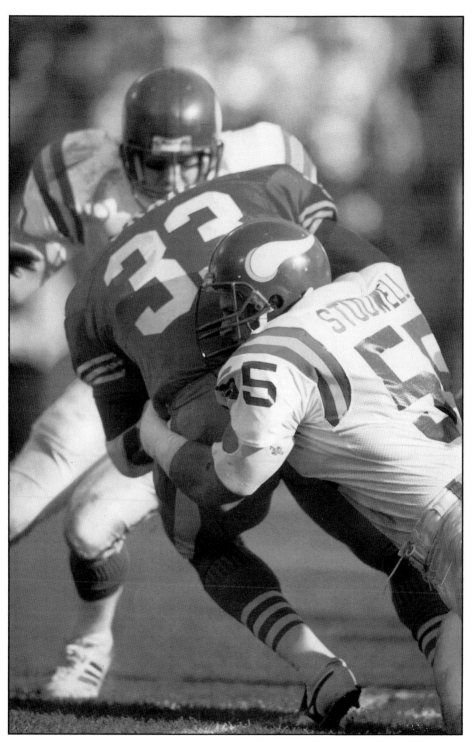

An all-time Viking great, Scott Studwell.

All-pro safety Joey Browner (#47).

The Vikings' #1 draft pick in 1987, D. J. Dozier.   31

1 9 9 1

Quarterbacks beware! Chris Doleman continued to be one of the NFL's greatest pass rushers.

A small man for pro football—Carter weighs only 175 pounds and stands 5'11"—he makes up for his lack of size with his "second sense" for the game. A sportswriter familiar with Carter's career wrote, "He just seems to know the right moves to make without even a second thought. It's instinct for him." Jerry Burns seconds that opinion, "I've always said that if the good Lord put anybody on this earth to play football, it was AC. He just forgot to give him a body."

Despite all this talent from Carter and the rest, the Vikings seemed to have difficulties realizing their potential. The late eighties and early nineties saw them return to playoff form, but they were unable to bring home the ultimate prize. Even the addition of Herschel Walker in 1989 couldn't get them to the top.

All of this promise, coupled with a long tradition of winning, however, may yet payoff in the 1990s. And there is nothing that would please the Vikings and their fans more than finally bringing home a Super Bowl victory to chilly Minnesota.